BIRDS

ANIMALS IN DISGUISE

Lynn Stone

The Rourke Corporation, Inc.
Vero Beach, Florida 32964

PHOTO CREDITS
All photos © Lynn M. Stone except—
© Peter James: pages 7, 21;
© Breck P. Kent: page 8 and small cover photo

EDITORIAL SERVICES:
Penworthy Learning Systems

Library of Congress Cataloging-in-Publication Data

Stone, Lynn M.
    Birds / Lynn M. Stone.
        p. cm. — (Animals in disguise)
    Includes index
    Summary: Describes how various birds use ways to disguise themselves and fool other animals, including camouflage and other tricks with color and shape.
    ISBN 0-86593-486-X
    1. Birds—Juvenile literature. 2. Camouflage (Biology) —Juvenile literature.
[1. Birds. 2. Camouflage (Biology)] I. Title II. Series. Stone, Lynn M.
Animals in disguise.
QL676.2.S76 1998
598.147'2—dc21
                                                                          98–6327
                                                                          CIP
                                                                          AC

Printed in the USA

TABLE OF CONTENTS

Birds   5

Staying Alive   6

Birds in Disguise   9

Camouflage   11

Birds on the Ground   14

Eggs and Chicks   16

Quick-Change Artist   19

Birds in the Reeds   20

Birds and Bluff   22

Glossary   23

Index   24

BIRDS

Birds are masters of flight. Their wings take them places where other animals can't go. But birds aren't always in flight. They need to feed, rest, find mates, and nest. Like other animals, birds face danger on the ground at times.

Birds **survive** (sur VYV), or stay alive, by **disguise** (dis GYZ). A disguise is a way of hiding or changing one's looks. Nature has given many birds ways to look like something other than birds.

Birds that feed and nest on the ground, like this African sand grouse, wear feathers that help hide them.

STAYING ALIVE

Most whippoorwills (WIP ur WILZ) are dull-colored birds. Their brown and gray feathers match the dead leaves of the forest floor. A whippoorwill resting in the leaves looks almost like part of the forest. Its colors help disguise the fact that it is a bird.

Being hard to see helps the whippoorwill escape the eyes of **predators** (PRED uh turz), the hunting animals. A predator can't catch a whippoorwill it doesn't see!

The chuck-will's-widow hunts insects at night, but it must hide on the leafy forest floor each day.

BIRDS IN DISGUISE

The whippoorwill depends upon the color of its feathers for safety. By blending with the forest floor, the whippoorwill increases its chances of survival.

When an animal wears colors that match its surroundings, the colors are called **cryptic** (KRIP tik). Cryptic colors help the whippoorwill and many other birds look like their surroundings. Birds like these **camouflage** (KAM uh FLAHJ), or hide, themselves in the objects around them. As long as the bird doesn't move or call, it can usually fool a predator.

A frogmouth's cryptic colors help it pass the day in Australia as part of a branch.

CAMOUFLAGE

Camouflage works best if a bird remains perfectly still. Sometimes a bird will sit still until someone or some animal is about to step on it.

One of the best camouflages is the golden plover's (see cover). Golden plovers spend summers on the Arctic **tundra** (TUN druh). The plover's brown, black, white, and gold feathers match the ground. That means the plover can hide from tundra predators.

On her nest, a female willow ptarmigan remains still—and almost unseen. 11

In cryptic colors of brown and gray, a nesting eider duck tries to hide among the willow branches.

A killdeer drags her wings to disguise herself as a wounded bird and leads a predator away from her nest.

BIRDS ON THE GROUND

The plover is a bird that ~~build~~

EGGS AND CHICKS

A sandpiper guards itself by blending into the world around it. Even the sandpiper's eggs are hard to see. They look like an artist painted them from the colors of the ground and plants nearby.

Some birds, such as terns, lay their eggs on beach sand. The dotted eggs disappear because they look like the sand.

Many chicks of ground-nesting birds use camouflage, too. The youngsters have cryptic colors, but they also lie low and still.

16

Seems like the golden plover's eggs and the dry tundra were painted by the same artist!

QUICK-CHANGE ARTIST

One of the bird masters of camouflage is the **ptarmigan** (TAHR mi gun). Ptarmigan are plump, chickenlike birds of the North. They feed and nest on the ground.

Each winter the ptarmigan wears white feathers. They are a perfect match for the snow.

When the snow melts in spring, the ptarmigan's white feathers are slowly replaced by brown! The brown coat keeps the ptarmigan camouflaged in summer. In autumn, white feathers again begin to replace brown.

Between summer and winter, a white-fronted ptarmigan wears a cryptic mix of colors.

BIRDS IN THE REEDS

Another master of camouflage is the bittern. This long-legged, long-necked bird hides in tall marsh plants.

Most animals lie flat to camouflage themselves. The bittern, though, stands tall. It may hold its bill straight up, too. Then the bird seems to be just another reed in the marsh. Sometimes the bittern even sways with the wind, just as the reeds around it do.

A bittern begins to raise its head so that it will stand like a reed in this Florida marsh.